£1.50

UNDER Candle BRIGHT

Poems and Reflections

Ian M. Houston

ISBN: 978-1-54399-613-5

eBook ISBN: 978-1-54399-614-2

Dedication

For my supportive and loving parents, Brenda and Allan Houston, and my siblings Glenn, Neal, and Leigh

For my encouraging Nana, Agnes Standbridge, and Granny, Winifred Houston

For my extended family- past, present, future

For special teachers, mentors, and friends

For my kind, thoughtful, fun-loving, and courageous children, Aidan, Griffin, and Grace, and their future partners and families

And, especially, for my dear wife and partner, Jolene 'Jo' Pendleton Houston, whose wisdom, humor, patience, faith, understanding, and love has been my inspiration and guide

Contents

The Imagined

There on hardened winter branches rest,
My lingering fears so firmly perched,
A returning omen in my breast
That this life may be cursed.

Have I so failed the test?
My weary eyes saddened,
It seems I have lost my zest,
My soul to shell am I resigned.

Then winds stir from the West,
Reassuring that I am not abandoned.
Onward with my continued quest,
Seeking for that which I imagined.

Forgotten Lass

Resting behind the museum glass
The stately royal gown.
A dress for but one class,
She who donned the crown.

No sign of the lovely lass,
From the Scottish farming town.
A name lost to museum brass,
She who stitched with such renown.

Grief, Allay

He, forsaken, molded words in clay,
Searching to create amidst the dim.
What healing spirit would grief allay,
Light to gathered blackness in him.

The pews were full they say,
Parted souls once burdened grim.
No longer shouldering the troubled day,
Such choirs sing a restful hymn.

Through windows, spring casts its ray,
This sorrow now poised to trim.
His hope often fell as prey,
Today it kept him above the rim.

Innocent Days

Faint elementary school recollections, that gentle strand,
Thieves of dear innocence do frequently swipe.
Often I keep shards of Cumberland,
Remember teachers who encouraged the imaginative type.
Sunnyvale was where my parents would land,
Far from British Isles and stirring bagpipe.
Coming to the Bay Area was unlike what they had planned,
But America was the bold, the brave, so went the hype.

In the school field, reaching so grand,
Stands the solitary tree, once so ripe.
There did I sit, climb, and stand,
Listen to friends who'd laugh and gripe.
Children of all grades there did band,
Under the branches, tears did I wipe,
When dearest Doug died, I ached to understand,
My innocent faith healed my heart's dark stripe.

Mother v. Demon

Scalding, always the spewing steam from his lips,
Behind the home door a family watched frozen.
Gulps from the bottle started as tumbler sips,
The Rye is his belly boiled as dark poison.

The children's hearts broken, filled with shattered chips,
Knowing it often came in dark winter season.
He raised rage, pulled leather from his hips,
Innocent, frightful eyes, searching for reason.

As his hand readied release of punishing whips,
Mother trembled, stood tall before the incensed demon.
No More! No More your anger that rips!
No Longer you take from children their freedom!

San Francisco Verse

Franciscan sainthood paled as hearts turned,
Eyes fogged by the bulging monied purse,
Minds jangling with coins, goals of gold churned,
Still, a breath of bay wind uttered a charitable verse.

Castles of wealth, soldiers deep for cash did march,
She was a captain descending below from the steel tower.
He lay shoeless with his dog under the stone arch,
His dreams long dashed, the desperate sign held so dour.

She crossed him, faintly catching his eye, hearing pleading voice,
No time, she thought, bridges to cross, battles for treasure awaited.
Yet, a whisper stopped her trek, and heartened a choice,
She stood for an instant, twisted, within her values debated.

Clear to her came what to do with ample cash accrued,
She entered the bakery, purchased drinks and warm bread,
The simple gifts to him she brought, his soul renewed.
Shined the city at the passage, kindness from hearts had not fled.

Footpath Bridge

I am at the end of Mill Street, my mind's grist in shaking hand,
I present to the mill, then her stones begin to grind my fears fine.
My swiftly passing life is not always as I had planned.

At the edge of the footpath bridge, now I stand,
The Occoquan pushes underneath with commanding design,
The flow holds me still, humbling is this procession grand.

Shall I cross the river in search of new land?
Does the circling hawk show in soft glide a sign?
I move forward, stopping halfway, my heart not one to demand.

I sense you here by my side, we of past and future do band,
A spot we did and shall as friends long line,
In common doubts each other we love, here together we understand.

The Mill Girls

The winter morn along Tay was especially dank,
Firm hands of thick dark choked the light.
Rising in chill were Dundee women few did thank,
To days that burdened life, they stood with fight.

To the jute mill, they gathered for meager wage,
They packed and pushed in with bairn by their side.
The clocked ticked start, the doors closed on the cage,
The drudgery so heavily weighed on their pride.

Days blurred past their eyes, to dusted lips came a voice,
The gaisgeil women in Scottish stubborn bold, said enough!
They met in dissenting quiet to plan their risky choice,
To stand naw faird before male owners who strutted so tough.

Dangers gathered, the greedy lords threatened their job,
The women rose united firm, knowing the tartan of their breed.
For fairness and justice, they firmly twisted the door knob,
And victory was theirs, to brave Mill Girls we bow, indeed!

Fallen Trees

Like strewn pens across a desk, rested fallen trees,
Weakened from weathered rot, yet, not inkless.
I combed my soul for what of loss they did profess,
My friend's farewell has brought me to my humble knees.

Upon my paper heart, they authored words to ease,
Striding deep into the grove, I confronted my mess,
I dwelt still, absorbed a truth they did confess,
At first listen, the verses did not for me please.

I desperately wanted my dear again here,
My spirit yearned, from my grey clouded eyes came rain,
So early, swiftly, my love taken far from me.

The fallen trees merely rested there, absent pain,
Their repose scrawled to me a line lacking fear,
Love peacefully breathes, from storms are we free.

Was It?

Was that God in
Pinstriped pressed suit,
With pockets overflowing gold?
Was it Him in top hat drawing
Clean lines across a sprawling
Paper map?
Were those Angels who
Built miles of stone wall,
Wired fences to divide?
Did Divine tug
The helpless child
From its fearful mother?
Did Rapture chain, enslave,
Whip, gas, tar and feather?
Did Heaven boisterously blow
Trumpets and polish swords
From which countless should die?
Was it Love that failed
To believe?

Lonely, Parted Luv

'I wonner whare ye now gaun'?
Said wee Jean, now 83.
'As sun light creeps ta dawn,
Do't somewhere shine on Archie?
I once haud your handsome brawn,
Whilst we strolled in Dundee.
I'm fair puckled, now often yawn,
But, oh, in luv, still me.'

Phillis, The Poet!

From West Africa her artful voice of splendor came,
A maturing inner soul was this girl's guide.
We shall steal her life, white men did proclaim,
Sinisterly shipped her across the treacherous tide.

Slave she was in the emerging nation's shame,
Alone, confused, this youthful saint surely cried.
In Massachusetts she was sold, Phillis Wheatley now her name,
She learned to read, her knowledge grew wide.

Then quilled pen the teen took, words sparked to flame.
The elite scoured her work, claiming she had lied!
A young African woman, a fraud the men would blame,
She knew the truth, prayed for her courage to abide.

The smug court of Hancock, Hutchinson treated her as game.
Reluctantly with arrogance they declared with no hint of pride,
The edified author, the enlightened African before them, the same.
Forward she went, enlightened gifts she did many provide.

The Ghost of Duncan

So roamed the poisoned ghoul of Duncan Avenue,
Once a man who did many hearts cut,
A soul no longer of any human hue,
Long since gone the life of gallus strut.

One damp night he haunted spaces he knew,
Passing Scotstoun Primary School, black iron gates shut,
He saw her spirit on Earlbank, standing true,
Halting his spook, the wife stirred the rat.

By her side, their four children in tow,
She crossed to him, and spoke at that,
Be still, we let your offences now go.
Forgiven, the ghost wept at the pains he begat.

Kansas City Welder

The faithful, Kansas City welder, the fighter from birth,
'Take in my 3rd grade daughter,' Oliver Brown said.
Monroe refused, 'Linda is not of the same worth.'
Never from such cruel verses would Oliver have fled.

Fire kindled in his eye, senseless injustice on earth,
No longer must hatred continue rearing its sinful head!
In wisdom he knew civil laws were deeply dearth,
He turned to the court, immorality they must be fed.

With wife, Leola, they braved thick racist girth,
Into the Supreme Court was the heartland case read.
Marshall arose, the 14th Amendment the fight was worth,
Nine agreed, racial segregation in schools had left its berth!

Loving Nana

Nana's Dover home edged near cliffs white,
Too slender for the car was the lane,
Mum steered through all the twists with fight,
Our tiny car battled the downpour of coastal rain.

Nana stood at the red door alone with a welcome,
She had just been baking shortbread biscuits,
Times without treats here so few and seldom,
Especially rich were the days of Christmas.

Her imaginative humour did make us giggle,
She would conjure funny voices, sing silly songs,
Then grab us with a hug and a tickle,
Never did she burden us with our wrongs.

El Carmelo Gardener

The Pacific Grove gardener mows the moist lawn,
To my shoes damp green clippings do stick.
He has nurtured El Carmelo Cemetery many days, dusk to dawn,
I am the guest beneath the Cypress trees settled on his proud turf thick.

Crossing me, he smiles gently, from my heart is grin also drawn,
Haphazardly, I read markers, not any of special pick.
Each name in me a placid thought is spawn,
Lives who walked as I, then seemingly ended all too quick.

The gardener's humming machine from my ears never withdrawn,
As I depart, he raises his hand with a warm, brief flick.
The peaceful earth by the sea this caretaker does so lovingly fawn,
Chiseled on his resting stone - *here an example that gentleness was no trick.*

Poem Never Published

I am the poem failed to be published,
I won't blame what my creator lacked,
Himself he too often has punished,
So many anxieties has he stacked.

I was penned with a hope of witness,
But I am not in any way bitter,
Such want is the human sickness,
I won't judge if I am crumpled into litter.

I will sit by and nurse my author,
Encourage him to churn me as he likes,
Finding my allusive shape can bother,
And, loyal am I when rejection again strikes.

Holding You Again

Forgive me, in life you always did,
Forlorn am I in this Westgate Garden.
These sundry years tug my drowsy eyes back,
Losing passion to look ahead,
Sleep does seem nearer.
You knew I was unhidden Love,
Who would not, did not, flee,
Never shielded my Yeatsian face?
Early I feared your beauty and kindness
Would attract the many, wiser, ampler than me.
Yet, you requited Love so, would bear more
For me than I ever could hoist for you.
I hearken the Bell Harry Tower bells,
Rings of joy were ever mine that you
Stayed with me as your charm grew,
Charitably letting me walk with you,
Encouraging verse for the chapters
Of your, of our book.
My heart does ache, my dear.
Though weary, each day I still
Reach for our pen,
While drying swiftly, some ink remains.
I lift the marker for you today.
I see you, sweet, in the red of
The tulip's bloom,
I hear you, soft, as the ducks glide
On the Great Stour,
I feel you, warm, on my face
Beneath the Kent sun.
Though I confess to more
Often looking back,
I still try to reach for the might,

To look onward,
Especially ahead to that hopeful day
Of holding Love,
Again.

Hero Stands

Aadila awoke in Arusha with ascending sun, polished her woman's armour,
Most days fear lurked, the fledgling family of six hanging by a strand.

She walked some distance, fetching what clean water she could garner,
Then scarce breakfast back to cook, children hungry in this Tanzanian land.

She and the village women harvested the ripe berries for the coffee farmer,
Working hours at the Kilimanjaro foot, to sweating face often her worn hand.

Having little comforts and possessions, she was not one to crave, to murmur,
By days end her frame ached, tomorrow she'd again be prepared to stand.

The Child Rises!

See that I am a starving child?
I will rise up!
Lock me in a border cage?
I will rise up!
Wrench my mother from me?
I will rise up!
Point a loaded weapon at my father?
I will rise up!
Leave me by the foul stench?
I will rise up!
Hear my sister's daily cough?
I will rise up!
When I have arisen,
I will teach my grandchildren
not to hate, read them Angelou.
I will tell them,
Turn to your neighbor,
See the lilies of the field,
Help humanity not despise, but
RISE up!

Dog Chewing Pen

Why do I stop you from chewing my pens?
You've likely considered the same question
When I pull them from you with anger in my voice.
I suppose I thought writing was a better use of them.
Sorry, was I so wrong.
I think you are on to something.
Here, take the entire box of rollerballs!
Take 'em all!
If I steal one from you to use, growl at me.
Even better, I'm coming under the table to chew with you.
Is that alright?
Can you teach me down there the joy of being genuine?

To Adventure

He was a youthful farmhand named Philippe Fleur,
Working the land of the wealthy Madame and Monsieur.
To him the autumn air of the French countryside was of particular allure,
He'd stop lifting the hay at moments, taking in the lands rolling contour.

He did, though, yearn for more, to what path he was rather unsure,
Came Theodore into his life, fresh with dreams, the young entrepreneur.
Theodore said follow me, and they'd find together in Paris fortune for sure,
Phillipe listened close, the adventure seemed to him so prosperous, secure.

He decided to leave, telling his fretful parents that too rousing was the lure.
The morning of farewell came, his sisters saw a knight standing so pure,
A tear swelled in his mother, she held her dear with loving assure,
Voice cracking, father smiled, remember my son, you once shoveled manure.

The Blades of Grass

The inconspicuous blades of midsummer grass
Are far better than me.
I hear no halting calls from them to passing feet,
No tangled refusals to be what they were created to be,
No craving of praise,
No assumption butterflies take notice,
Not one demand that moisture fall.
These creations are neither
Rooted in greed nor, as I,
Carrying thorns of pride.
With respite, I do pause here in my flaws,
Attentively watch from the open window,
Gather wisdom from blankets of green.

Furry Fluff

Awoken was the four-legged creature from
His snooze,
The hefty, furry fluff, sniffed the castle looking
For clues,
To many rooms he searched for delectable items
To choose,
Finding his love, his mouth watered, saliva
Did ooze,
He had found in the darkened closet his master's smelly
Old shoes.

Liberating Day

He entered the majestic hall with characteristic bluster,
Discordant words filled the room in lingering smoke.

Loyal, smartly suited staff in corners did cluster,
Blind ambition fed by he in foul cloak.

The people gathered, sharp opposition did they muster,
Crying, no more loathing that he does stoke.

They witnessed hate was his fund as trustor,
He placed round their necks a heavy darkened yoke.

Then the liberating day arrived in morning luster,
His divisive voice now departed, valleys again awoke.

Falls of Dochart

Our mysteries deep beneath River Dochart flow,
We, the injured soul, pacts with life we seek.

By soothing Falls, Killin winds faintly blow,
Our blackened boulder breast is what styles us meek.

Together, we as guests of nature's show,
Gather on the stone bridge, bruised spirit, path bleak.

What ashes in waters shall we throw?
Perhaps we hold firm that which makes us weak.

In this humility, we are human so,
As pure as the river which never words speak.

Heartbroken Daughter

In the valley of numberless green striped field,
Was the tiny white house, prison-like, dirty.
Workers crowded, rent paid with what they could yield,
Sharing beds and two bathrooms were souls thirty.

Ana just turned fifteen, fresh womanhood sealed.
Families met for her Quinceañera party,
They carried much food, special gifts they could weald.
Young and old, sang, laughed, prayed, there the warm army.

Ana's doting papa, Ricardo, was her valiant protector,
When disheartened, she turned to him most.
The single father's gentleness was often her needed nectar,
He gifted her a birthday diary, giving to her with no tears, almost.

Ricardo knew her talents, how written words did affect her,
He dreamt she'd reach beyond the picking fields of the coast,
That she'd walk the ivy halls, stand with the university rector,
It was a wish they together shared, a path for growth, not boast.

When the house was sleeping, came loud knocks on the door,
Men with badges burst, yelling of staying he's not worthy!
They found Ricardo, under a blanket, frozen on the floor,
Ana had never seen him afraid, his voice pleading for mercy.

Away from his family torn, tattered clothes are all he wore.
Months passed, Ana's weeping heart beat ink into her diary,
Writing for her father's love she longed, a human at her core.
She stood tall for their dream, even when valley days were dreary.

Myself Forgive

The drying river never blamed the sun,
The broken branch never accused the wind,
The fallen pedal never questioned the rain,
The webbed fly never impugned the spider,
Why my troubled heart does blame,
Wrestling with my guilt to forgive?

From Afar

Your cheeks glitter amidst the golden frill,
Your words soft downs fluttering by fountains grand,
Your eyes sparkle when silver's spun,
Draw out you, the dazzling red in tabled roses.
I watch your beauty luster with the celebrating crowd.
Yet, I am sorry, I should not, cannot stay.
Forgive me as I slip away, my love,

It is simply that I should always hold you back,
I am not that beaming star you are,
You are the light, I am the darkness,
I am the taker, weak, you are the giver, strong.
Know I shall celebrate your talents,
Cherish, you, darling, your shine
From afar.

Widegates Charity Tale

Each day, across the Cornwall seasons,
Clive, an aged, grey bearded farmer
Walked alongside Widegates fields, up and back.
He pondered as he passed through chiseled,
Winding paths of tall hardened hedgerow,
Channels he knew so well.

At his side was Staples,
A devoted sheepdog with
Long shining coat of silky white and black.
As they gently strolled, often breezes whistled,
Sheep, cows, birds each uttered pure
Messages, nature's songs to tell.

Clive would often stop at the Tredinnick Farm Shop,
Purchasing eggs, milk, modest
Items the two did lack.
He befriended there, Lewis, a kind young store hand,
Local to Hessenford, quiet,
With no arrogance to sell.

They relished Lewis, and he so them,
Together exchanging thoughts, strokes, laughs,
As Lewis carefully filled the sack.
One rainy Cornish day, Lewis said to Clive,
"My Mum has passed," tears
Down freckled cheek did fell.

Clive extended his tender hand,
"Dear lad, death cuts we who stay,
I know hope yearn her back."
Said Lewis, *"Last night I went into*
The dark chill, angry, far into
The open field to yell."

His coat dripping rain, Clive embraced Lewis,
Staples pulled close,
This young man such grief his heart did pack.
Next morn, Clive picked wild flowers, presented to his friend,
With such gracious charity,
Lewis' sadness lifted, struggled to dwell.

Duty Calls, Tomorrow

Duty, your rich tenor draws me near,
Time after time.
I will be one striving to pay homage
To your heroic lines,
For in you is the
Purposeful, rewarding life of wisdom, of service.

Yet, please, be not disapproving of me
As today I turn away,
Closet you up along side
The obligations, tasks, commitments,
Each that dangle in this cabinet of life.

Forgive me, today I shall stroll
With the sheep on the idyllic
Carpet of hillside green,
Here, I am away from the village
Near the glimmering lake
Where water graces boats.

I shall, I hope, tomorrow,
Be loyally dressed,
Upright,
Polished
For you,
Just not today.

Rest Under Rowan Tree

Bent on battered knees,
She wept under the Rowan tree of North Fife,
Shivering in autumn dark, anxious for
Magic power to lift her cloud of strife.
Out came the sharp sgian-dubh, to tender heart
Demons lay the chilled knife.

The breeze rustled the leaves,
The voice of the goddess came to life.
'Don't run from struggle,' the berried tree sung,
'Face troubles in you rife.'
Such melodies could not save the fair lass,
There to rest came the despairing wife.

The Chipping Campden Grave

Outside St. James is the unmarked wooden grave,
Resting stump, not etched - *here lies breast brave,*
Once a solitary tree, did praise never it crave,
Limbs for singing birds is what it gave,
Never did it preach within the church nave,
Critique souls aloud, judge the paths some pave,
Though, but wordless, selfless life, did it behave,
With arching splendor did poorly hearts it once save.

The Comforter's Key

Worry does spin, swirl, trouble, much weaken me,
It comes often to claim a costly fee.
From this darkness I earnestly pray to flee,
Comfort holds in hand the worn gate's key,
He twists it so, then sets me free.

Accepting Hold

The moment was as an open field of crisp summer gold,
Now standing at the harvest edge, his heart, once empty, cold.
He knelt before her, *'Please have me until I grow old?'*
She beamed widely, teared, taking his trembling hand in accepting hold.

Shelley Sing

The parochial powers of old accused you of damaging slur,
Expelled you, the outspoken bold, the brashest.

You, their precious prey, as plump cats they did purr,
Though, your words have survived the Oxford inquest.

Still the hypocrisy, injustices, we humans do truth so blur,
Yet the joyful skylark melody ever springest.

At this pond, Percy, you sing with creatures that stir,
Nature's melody shall always surpass the dishonest.

Environment Save

In the jungle of the savage streets,
Clad in green, pad in hand,
She youthfully looked me in the eye, courteously asked,
"Do you have time for the environment?"
"I do, I do, indeed, ink my name," said I.
'Save the Environment' we agreed
As the city buzzed around us.

Then part I did with certain thoughts befriending me.
Protect the creatures, the birds,
Root your feet by the grove of arching trees,
Cleanse the soiled water,
Lace the walking shoes,
More often cast aside
Those ignition keys!

But so, too, this thought
Was winged to me,
To chill the arctic sea by one degree
May prove beyond my humble grasp to see.
Yet within certain reach
Were the words of love
For those souls closest to me.

A kind word for them
Would swing from the trees,
Swoop from the sky,
Emerge from core to clean air,
Then stir within and ease their troubled heart
By one, by two,
Perhaps, three degrees.

Returned for Moment

Today, older, I am again at the foot of the clay,
The Provo white tower bell again a ringing beacon.
Here a path led, while younger, forgiving my errant way,
Stirred in me were tastes, words for my soul that did sweeten.
I knelt then, aiming to reconcile past and present in prayerful ballet.

Still, so often I was unable, alone, I perceived myself beaten.
A grander sketched plan never rendered for me to stay,
Forward I went, carrying a mind that seemed fully awoken.
Sobering since has been the journey, though rich with joyful ray,
I see a shadow on the campus lawn, for him my heart weakens.

Nesting Angel

Doubt often allures out
The fragile and lonely shadows in me.
Then feathered wings of words
Gently brush my cheek.
Fear, she chirps,
Is a time for courage,
An hour for mild hearts to sore,
A moment where tender eyes
May open to light and bloom.
An angel again is nesting here
Amidst the murky soul that
Often stirs in me.

The Father of Fishers

He watched his brave sons ascend the brae,
Then away they were from their boyhood sea.
A father's soul longed for them to stay,
He was the ancient fisherman named, Zebedee.

Proud of their courage each passing day,
He knew a singular mission had led them to flee.
Alone now mending nets, he was earnest to pray
For James and John, who had departed Galilee.

A man showed Zebedee's sons and many the way,
Love for others He exclaimed was the journey's key,
Turn from the lurers of pride, keep hatred at bay.
Forgiveness permeated the man's eyes and graceful plea.

Farewell Son

Here is where the innocent stream,
The sparkling fresh river each
Greet the radiant sea,
A fleeting but genuine estuary where past and future
Fondly embrace.
It is a hallowed spot between father and son,
Between eternal friends such as you and me.
As you turn to the breeze and courageously hoist your
Promising sail to the ocean's wondrous call,
Listen to me here as I sing a song of joy,
Hear the notes of deep pride in you,
Forgive my shaking voice, for these thoughts of farewell have
For so long swelled in me.

Hillside Grass

Tall brown grass hidden away,
High up the hillside am I,
Far from the spinning fray,
Never asking the reason why.

Thus told where to stay
And shant leave, or even try,
Neither to dream of someday,
Nor possessing such eyes to cry.

Troubles Below

I shall place my fears
At the foot of the climb
Then venture upwards slowly in time.
Through the mud I go,
Over the rocks, ford the streams,
Pass under the leafless branches.

Then stand shall I atop the hill
As winter winds leave dried grass unstill.
My breast is aglow,
For no longer
I see those troubles
left below.

Together

I shall one day shed the dust,
Glide with the mentoring angels
Just above the tips of the trees.
There I shall await you.

Though, wings are not yet hatched,
My hand still lovingly is yours,
Our feet together have still much
Delightful earth to cross.

Til Journey's End

She awoke teeming with unease,
Just as she had the day before,
And days before that.
Through ritual she arose,
Moved to beautify what was already beautiful,
Though not to her.
Gathered in her colorful layers,
Standing at the gate to step out
Again unto the track,
She paused,
Closed her lonely hazel eyes,
And took a deep breath.
Then she was off, turning right,
Down the street.

He, too, with long disquieted breast
Rolled from his intermittent sleep,
Moving slowly to prepare,
Selecting unconfidently what to wear.
He pulled his necktie tight,
A red and blue stripped noose,
He fleetingly thought.
He stood at the door,
Leather shoes laced up,
Held his hand over his bearded face,
Whispering a cry that sprung from
His brooding, forlorn soul.
Then he was off, turning left,
Up the street.

Though unknown to one another,
They were neighbors in grief.
Their heads were up,

Looking ahead as they approached.
When they crossed,
Each shyly turned
Their eyes away, slightly down
In their silent pain,
Strangers avoiding any greeting, any smile.
Then she stumbled
When her heal caught the city grate,
Causing her shoe to be displaced.
He stopped,
Turned when hearing her voice.

It was a hesitant, modest question
He posed,
"Are you alright?"
As she wiggled her pump
Firmly back in place,
She looked him in the eye,
"Yes, thank you, yes I think so."
There they stood, strangers no more,
Anguish beginning to lift.
Then they were off, neither turning left nor right,
Neither up nor down,
But crossing the street,
Together,
Til journey's end.

Winged Theatre

Angelically, across
The stage of a blue grey sky
She danced.
The tips of her wings were pink,
Spotlighted by a rising winter sun.
I had come to the Virginia theatre,
No ticket, no cost, no crowd.
In her exquisite flight
Resplendent grace was given
Imperfect me.
Then beyond my sight she was,
Alas, soaring to another lowly heart
She went.

Powdered Keg

Wullie Laird was an auld, beld Glesga man
A blethering seafaring dug with ae wooden leg.
He wad cladder herty stories of his sailor's clan,
Ev'n more as young bright fu' mates wid beg.

Blootered tales aboot cauld seas tae huners a fan,
Wullie stuffed with pub tatties, sad sangs, how cum his peg.
The ship gang from Hielan, aw wis guanae tae plan,
Then Bang! The de'il had gaen blasted the powdered keg.

Pillowless Prince

Aging, frail soul,
You of long grey beard,
Weathered skin.
You, who harmlessly sleep,
Pillowless,
Coverless,
Atop a sliver of cardboard,
Nestled in corners of empty lots.
As the city rises,
With all its shining trinkets and shimmering toys,
So different shall be your autumn day to mine.
Be still, hold forth sweet stranger,
Brother, son of God.
Charity may allude you today, tomorrow,
Soon cold late season nights descend,
Winter begins to stir from its slumber and awaken.
Heaven knows of you,
Lovingly hungers and prepares for your royal return,
Angels are set to raise your regal banner!
You, the Sacred Heart,
You, the Pillowless Prince, who carry burdens in life,
Which so few have gallant mite to bear!

A Celestial Piece

There went a part of my soul
When he left this life,
Not to vanish,
But walk by his side,
A celestial piece of me
Now already strolls with him
In the heavens above.

The City Pigeon

I am not the stately eagle that soars,
Turning the heads of admirers.
I am neither the brave hawk whose cry
Shrieks from the sky, nor the prancing peacock
Whose colors dazzle the eye.
I am the lowly, city dwelling pigeon,
With not much for flight,
For imperial plumage,
For striking chords.

They will say I am bland, a pest,
Feeble, bobbing my neck,
Timidly begging for crumbs.
Though, still, I am who I am,
Live as I can only live,
Created to comfort as I may comfort,
And give as I may give.
Alas, that is me,
The city pigeon.

Into the Golden Wood

Teacher settles the room.
The morning roll is read.
Pewter Inkwell?
'Full and moistened!'
Parchment Paper?
'Clean and unmarked!'
Quilled Pen?
'Sharp and tempered!'
Mahogany Desk?
'Shinning and dusted!'
Upright Chair?
'Warm and cushioned'
Author M. Be?
Author M. Be?
Author?
Then out the window teacher glances.
In thrillful run so goes,
Author Might Be –
Into the golden autumn wood
In search of light,
Of life,
Of peace.
All breathlessly await her return!

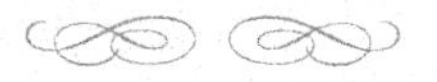

Scottish Bard

The wee heart of that panicked
Timid beastie of bare Ayrshire autumn field,
Ruined housie under dominion's plough,
It called out to me through her winged cousin's toil,
A restoration of nature's social union to see.
She intensely stuffed forest twigs with artful industry
Just as the mothering mouse prepared
To dwell cozily for weary winter.
I have learned from you, my Scottish bard,
Listened to the guilt that day when
Horse drawn blade with no willful intent
Spoiled the best of innocent schemes.
I carefully hold back the tampering
Human hand in honour of you, my inspiration.
I follow thy ways and whisper
To the blessed bird as thou to the blessed mouse,
I tell her be free, just be.
I will not do harm, and encourage others the same.
There will be no words of your
Backward eye of prospects dreary.
Hearts like mine now aim to sing of kindness
Because of what delightful soil your soulful pen unearthed.
I entreat in tribute to thee, Robert, my friend,
That such plans this mother has of spring may bloom,
And that you, and the wee beastie of long ago,
Shall have joy in what is now your field,
Your realm of deserving rest.

Future Nourished

She did not lack a dream, a wish on her lips,
There was no shortage in him of a lively smile.
They were children, siblings awaking in a village,
Giggling on the dirt floor as they prepared for the day.

A placid morning voice led the children to task,
The young mother with no work, a husband lost to war,
Abundant was her love for her delicate family,
Never scarce affection, warm words plentiful.

They sat still for a moment and bowed in grace,
Each morning grateful for what they had and for hoped.
As regular as faith, so also the daily routine of no food.
With dreams and smiles, they strode to school.

There they saw village women mixing large pots,
Singing as they stirred the warm porridge.
The children mingled with friends, patiently awaiting,
Into the blue mug breakfast came, a meal, a human right.

Nourished, the children walked into the school,
Heard whispering the sister to her brother,
'One day a doctor I would like to be, just wait and see.'
Teacher wished all a good morning, time to learn, to grow.

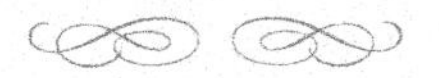

The Leaf

Who am I
To receive what
Rapture bestows,
The singular pass
To witness this recital of your
Delicate dance?
The stage lights rise,
In rusted red you softly spin,
Pirouette farewell through
The season's breeze.
You would not see,
You would not feel,
What joy,
What wonder
My soul draws from thee.
Ah, that I wish I could return
To you what your waltz has
Brought to me.

I Will Stay

I stood at the open window,
Watched the curtain moving,
The hem of the angel's gown.
She softly danced on the
Frame seal.
She seemed on the edge,
To stay, to float away.
'Should you wish to depart'
I woefully said,
'Please do.'
'No, I shan't leave
you alone,
I shall remain here
with you,
swaying together
with to the music of the city below,'
she said.

For A Royal Leamington Walk

Two up and down, terraced brick,
The theatre of ten royal souls.
Motionless, the children lay
Within the night dark.

A damp chill sustains ringing coughs.
Fevered infant, dear, clings
To mother's dry cracked breast.
No doctor.

Penny, simple George V
Copper coin, does allude.
The open mouth, the slot,
Belly of the gas meter again goes unfed.

Under candle bright,
Father with shaking hands
Removes the valves, twists off bottom caps,
Slips off the slides of the cornet.

Mixing soap with rain water,
He dips his brush,
Then in and out of the valves he goes.
Then reassembles his joy.

With rag in hand,
Father's breath puffs beneath
His dark mustache.
The brass then so shines.

The grey blanketed sun rises,
Though his eyes never rested.
Eldest daughter in
Torn knickers is now up.

Please, play father, she asks.
Then siblings rise
To her voice.
Father puts his hand to their heads.

Tis' too early, my lovelies,
He tranquilly says.
He gathers his tattered coat, hat, scarf,
Clutches the shimmering cornet.

Unto Chandos Street goes he,
Down Warwick, left on Parade,
Right on Regent, striding to the pawnbroker.
His soul pauses, his feet yield at the door.

To the back he treads,
Comes face to face with the old man
Already with tobacco pipe.
I wish to sell this, he says.
The manager takes hold, assesses.

The deal is done.
Pocket full, father walks past the tempting pub.
To his family he returns,
A man with conflicted heart.

Now all are awake, greet him with joy.
Mother with infant in arms
Asks him to whence he'd gone.
For a walk, my darling, his loving reply.

Park Bench Sparrows

Sweet, delicate creatures
Edge forward,
Please, fear not.
Let me tend to thee,
For what am I, but wingless weight?
Earth grounded by human pride?
Take here what I have in hand,
For faith utters to me
That thou hast been sent,
Hath gracefully flown from above
To teach me gentle lessons
Of hope,
Of healing,
That I could not, never, so
Exquisitely instill.

The Knight Hand

It was a hole in her soul,
Leaking desire.
He gracefully took his wrinkled hand,
Softly placed it
Over the vent of his queen's waning heart,
Promising her
With a noble whisper to hold it so,
A shield of armor,
Until her last breath.
Farewell, sweetest Love.

Lonesome Fisherman

The odor of squid never left his well-worn hands,
The bait was the Monterey wharf fisherman's defining scent.
Once wounded in war, his scars no soul understands,
Boyhood innocence to distant jungles of blood it went.

He places his tattered Giants cap over grey strands,
Departs his tiny home just more than a tent.
He carries pole and tackle, limping slowly up beach sands,
Assuming the weight of a lonely life in final decent.

Unto the wharf, to his chosen spot he lands,
Into the ocean his baited hook is downward sent.
He no longer of life has any joyful demands,
Just for the red snapper nibble, this broken heart content.

Goodbye, Dearest Friend

Sweetest comfort
Was you
When some days drifted dark.
Our loyal companion to hold,
To softly stroke,
To whisper to
When life clenched a fist.
There you were as this family,
This continuing joy,
Bustled and burst.
Let me now
With shaking hand
Slowly slip this lead
From you.
Did we bring but
One measure
Of what you quietly
Delivered us?
Accept this gentle kiss.
Let us see your kind eyes
Open one last time
Then find mellowed rest.
Farewell dearest friend,
Run now,
Be truly free.
We will think of you in the woods
As God's innocent creatures
Teach us,
To pray,
To love,
To be.

Her Courageous Light

For miles
She shouldered the peat,
The water, the maize,
The fowls, the fruit,
The vegetables,
Golden grain.

Her blistered feet ached,
Hands sore,
Her face burnt
From the sun,
Skin cracking from
The brisk breeze.

She skinned the fish,
Lit and extinguished the fire,
Spun the creaking spinning wheel,
Swept the dirt floor,
Nurtured the children
Often alone.

She anxiously waited on shore
For the fishing boats to reappear
From the stormy sea.
She prayed for wars to end,
For innocent
Sons, fathers, brothers, husbands to return.

She then went to sleep,
But not for long,
She fittingly awoke before the
Morning rays,
She was the courageous light
Ready to start, again.

Saint of Water Leith

I stood up from the right bank bench,
Leaned over the edge alongside St. George's Well,
A witness to the imagined regalia
Of your long white apron serenely swaying with
Autumn leaves down Water of Leith.
You had toiled in once these surrounding droning mills,
Before dawn, after dusk.
As you laboured, so, too, did your precious children,
And demanding, howlin' husband,
Scant wages for all, barely enough to stay afloat.
Yet, you still came back, again and again,
Strength of soul, bonnie smile that warmed the grey,
Dashes of rose across your hardened, freckled cheeks,
Ginger locks on your shoulders did rest.
Here I am under the luxury of soothing repose,
There goes your cloth gliding further down the river,
Across the polished rocks, toward St. Bernard's Well.
Where is your monument?

Young Russian Artist

The solitary young woman
Knelt with the white canvass,
Began delicately pulling out
Her brushes and paint.
She seemed to be searching
On the park path.
When asked if perhaps one day
We could see the finished work,
She said with quiet reticence,
'Oh no, I am not yet good enough.'
As we parted,
I glanced back
Witnessing before me
Not simply the artist,
But the painting itself,
A young life more than
good enough,
One to be known,
One to be cherished.

Pirate's Tale

Captain Whippit stood before the boisterous crew,
His silver cup running over with spiced rum,
With garish howl from his belt the cutlass he drew,
Such fright he slashed in hearts with great aplomb.

Fowl was his heart, thick upon it the layer of scum.
As the angry sea, in him violence would often stew,
To the cry of suffering he had become numb,
His soul blackened, more sailing in darkness there were few.

As he lay in his cabin holding a ruby he had forgotten where from,
He reached for another sip of his poisoning brew,
Candle flickering, a seafaring song he did give raspy hum,
Looking out upon the moonlit sea, there arose a green spirit in view.

Into his cabin it entered with a whiz and swoosh of great sum,
It's eyes so bright, like the tip of fire burning vivid blue!
Whippit, quaking hand to his face, asked from whence had it come?
The spirit refused, saying, 'I am here to ask what has become of you?'

He lifted his flintlock that had been the grave to some,
The spirit cusped its lips, into the waters the pistol it blew.
Whippit lay motionless, feeling death was surely the outcome,
Said the spirit, her charge to break the pirate's heart to be laden with rue.

The spirit raised a webbed hand, Whippit's thieving tongue did she dumb,
Leaving him a choice to put behind the horror he did spew.
He there made a pledge, no more would he beat the terror drum,
He wept in shame, then chartered a charitable course anew.

The Metro Smile

He dutifully edges forward, head down.
Footprints mark the descending path,
Lead to this worn rostrum of crowded loneliness.
He numbly stands ready in place
As early morning he has often before.
The metal curtains draw open,
Without intent a spark rekindles in him
When her lonely eyes meet his.
Their eternal meaning awoken
When through the clangs, dingdongs,
He, unrehearsed, greets her,
She blinks slowly,
Ever so slightly, she *smiles.*

Pedaled Path

Never forgotten these shared sorrows we hath,
Patches I collect, stitch with silken thread.
Now lined with pink pedals our path,
Together we shall press forward, peace ahead.

Rain Drop

Would it be greedy of me
To open my hands in want,
Catch you in my palms as you descend,
Feel the heaven from above?
Or be it meek to clasp my hands in prayer,
Not impede your fall,
See you complete a divine journey
To the soil that has for a season
Thirsted your touch?

Sea Shell

It was your time to hold life
Deep beneath the mighty sea.
Now free on this patch
Of hallowed earth,
You rest,
After being what you were
Designed to be.
Never lost,
Never prideful,
Never doubting.
Time is still with me to ask:
What story shall accompany my fragile shell?
What heavenly shore shall I soon
Come to freely sleep upon?

Her Lesson Song

When winter softly brushes
The fallen autumn bronze,
An angelic morning wood sings,
Her awakening voice crisp, so calm,
There are seasons for all things,
So goes her ancient song.

Charity of Letters

I pull out this letter "O"
From my mind's shallow pocket,
Spin the ring around my finger,
Place it over my head,
Fashion a necklace,
Fling it as a frisbee across a field,
Roll it along the street.
What more is there to do?
What meaning alludes this toy
Before back in the pocket it goes?
Then sitting face in hands is the
Unsteady, ragged man on the park bench,
Bookends of tied black plastic bags enclosing him.
Surrounding him are letters as well, yet not for play.
An H in his beaten eyes,
An E in his torn shirt,
An L in his ragged shoes,
An L by his cup partially full
with a smattering of coins.
My O I hold to my mouth,
Then latch it to those letters shadowing him.
Out comes the simple creation from my lips,
"hello."

Other Passages

Under waves of shame, does he drown,
Near Walton Lighthouse does David muse,
Far from home, his simple Kansas town,
The addict suffers in Santa Cruz.

Shadowing failure is what pulls him down,
The needles, heroin, paper bags of booze,
He who once dreamt of musician renown,
Many years he played, paying his dues.

Stepping out, seeing no passing witnesses around,
Heart blackened, hidden ink of lowly tattoos,
Thinking never to wear a golden crown,
Flickering to an end his candle fuse.

'I'm sorry,' he whispered with tearful frown,
Edging into the water with tattered shoes,
The lighthouse, the angel in white gown,
Preaching in green light, other passages to choose.

Woman of Urban Courage

Within these chiseled concrete caves,
She awakens again long before
The morning chime.
She rubs her face in the darkness,
A lonely hand,
A temperate touch,
Only she can now provide.
A tear wells,
a stream runs ahead of her wind of whispered words,
'I can't do this.'
Then angels of hope lift and stir an ore,
Pilot her forward from her bed.
She clasps her hands,
Faithfully faces another day,
As saintly medals are molded, casted,
Dipped in gold,
Just for her.

The Stonemason

I would audibly call out the roll,
Sing names out boldly for others to hear,
Though most remain unknown to me.
The stonemason's unwritten canon prefers it such.
The *art overshadows the name* they chisel in the air.
I celebrate this elegant chorus of nameless craftsmen.
I close my eyes and imagine the leathered,
Frayed hands of a master at his trade.
Gratitude is notched in me.

The Genuine

Shall I accept the offer?
Slip off my shoes
At the edge of the season's loosening embrace?
Step into the stream
Before it chills?
Feel the smooth river stones below my feet?
If I had but one piece of
The tree's authenticity,
Casting aside my falsehoods,
What peace to find?
If I could perform lyrics
By this brook, this yellowing wood,
Sing like the divine voices of gentle autumn birds,
What comfort be mine?
I am a pretender, they, the genuine.

Deep Mined Love

Awoken early to Hera's cries, their fresh divine infant,
The helpless child who slept close by their bedside.
Baby soft, smooth cheeks wholesome of Cornish heath pigment,
The Truthwall parents giggled, whispered dreams with blooming pride.

Precious morning time together so passed in an instant,
William clothed, left to mine, labouring for his bride,
Looking down Levant Road, his breast this day resistant,
Though courage he had mustered before light touched tide.

Gwenna remained behind with child, ample chores never scant,
To cottage duties, she the young strong mother tied.
The coastal autumn days did shine, so radiantly enchant,
Though tempted, never from her duty did she hide.

The Great War had ended, horror hushed the chant,
Levant Mine stumbling, though still bustling, stirring tin inside,
Workers mined their fear, such blackness did generously grant,
Up and down, the Man Engine did unsteadily slide.

Dust, noise, family images from William would never supplant,
Though in the skinny shaft, dreams, tragedy did collide.
As he and labourers emerged up with miner's fervent,
Link between rod and engine snapped, men screamed, died.

News spread, villagers cried, 'men taken so, God can't!'
Gwenna stood by clothes she hung, not yet dried,
The Vicar came, the reasons struggling to be conversant,
Gwenna frighteningly alone, trembled, 'where dost he now abide?'

Aged, Hera returned to Levant, wearing a silver pendant,
Given to her late mother with hopeful love supplied,
William had pledged his heart, eternal affection, glowingly resplendent,
Hera gazed out, the glimmering Celtic Sea she eyed.

Standing by cliffs, light rain Hera gave little regard,
Her family, granddaughter, Gwenna, stood lovingly by her side,
From disaster many years past came hurtful shard,
To Hera the consoling light, never shall tenderness subside.

Mr. Rose

I may stand erect, crimson bold,
Draw to me your admiring eye,
Pull in your fingers to hold.
Yet I am weak, embracing a lie,
Peel back my delicate petals cold,
See selfish doubt, love me, why?

Emerson's Grief

Ellen often rocked in the cushioned red chair,
She read, pondered, warmth did she lovingly share.
Graceful beauty circled her face, so elegantly fare,
To her, his ardent love, would Ralph declare.

Behind her teenage eyes, passion did flair,
He repeatedly stopped, looked her way to stare.
They wed in New England, a handsome pair,
Many a friend so pleased to be there.

Soon came to her tuberculosis, the dark affair,
He leaned on his faith in earnest prayer.
She could not stay, to God his glare,
Grieved, he began to doubt His divine care.

To nature he traveled, searched in transcendental despair,
There in time he found a peace beyond compare.
On his heart tarnished faith did he wear,
Though hoped of angelic Ellen was God aware.

The Blue Magic

Oscar was practicing alone in the summer twilight,
An unsettled golfer searching for what would keep him returning.

He peered over the pond at the pin, fancying the links highlight,
Then selected his stick, the 7-iron, like him, rusted face, but still breathing.

He took aim, struck the turf fat, into the hazard went the Titleist white.
Leaning by the water's edge, Oscar began his standard surgical probing.

Under the shimmering glass, he spotted a brilliant blue pill bright,
He reached down and pulled out the ball in his hand now gleaming.

The ball beamed and whispered, 'play me before day yields to night.'
He raced to the next tee, his tattered game needed no convincing.

Oscar teed up, with a mighty swipe whacked the blue ball out of sight.
He rushed forward, found it at rest 2 feet from the cup, blue jewel pulsating.

Heart full of joy, he tapped in for eagle, his effort ever so slight.
The blue ball was magic, his trophies and wealth would soon begin amassing!

The next hole an ace! He kissed the smiling ball with bursting delight,
He broke out in elated dance, this game no longer would he be fighting.

Then he heard his name shouted, a punch on his arm gave him a fright,
His wife cried out, 'Oscar, wake up, it's time for working, not dreaming!'

The Scented Scripture

I momentarily turn my thoughts away
From the voices inside the walls of the church.
I peer through the window at a lean preacher
Clad in green, capped in shades of pink.
Her elegance pulls me up from the creaking pews,
A wordless sermon is the sweet pollen that feeds my hunger,
Her beauty propels me out past mahogany doors.

I am not alone here by her side,
Other small parishioners crawl around,
Fly about under puffs of white and a vault of blue.
I lean in, confess my doubts.
In her scented splendor she ministers to me
With a restoring scripture,
Nothing so lovely could be of man.

Breathed

I, too, rested by the humming stream,
Listened to the birds invite one another,
Witnessed twilight sprinkle an enchanting,
Glistening dust upon the water.
I was once here, alert to life as you,
Balancing doubts, distrust, and fears
Alongside faith, confidence, and courage.
I am now together in rest with those
Who also stood there long before me.
They have told of a message so often whispered to me.
And so with them, I bring it to you.
Hear it in the subtle winds that softly rustle the trees,
Feel it in the smooth stone resting in the river bed,
See it in crested blue iris that line the water's edge.
Inhale the grace of precious life.
And when you stand from your rest by the stream,
Walk toward those whom you love without hesitation,
Stroll with a renewed glimmer in your eye.
Hold them close.
Share with them what you have
Breathed in on this day.

A Parent's Work

The spinning,
The weaving,
The wefts,
And warps,
Aching hands seaming through the loom.
To what end?

Then the velvet royal tapestry
Is unraveled before me
In all its knotted
Regal richness.
I catch my breath
Seeing what it has become.

I shall carry this creation,
Drape it upon my shoulders,
Pull it across a veil,
Hoist it up on the wall of
A palace above.

I shall forever admire that
A graceful,
Merciful hand
Showed far more artistry
Than I could
Ever stitch.

The Water's Layer

I so effortlessly break through
The thin layer of glimmering glass.
My fingers, hand, soul,
All alert to the soothing residue
Of once a winter snow,
Now melted, rushing by.
As easily as I reached in, I lift out,
Close my eyes, splash my aging face.
The breeze, spring air are companions
Drying the moment as soft towels.
Tranquil, humbled, I open my eyes.
I see before me a regalia of colors,
All singing notes from nature's songbook.
Opened for me long ago was the gift of life,
Still I celebrate it though time is
More precious and fleeting now.
Why now gifted this breath of life?
I stand upright from the stream
With what strength I have still been granted,
Searching, turning thankfully toward
The guiding light.

Across the Veil

I walked alone this morning,
Looked out on an azure sky,
Across an emerald field.
I was surrounded by a chorus of
Singing birds.
There I met your wrinkled grin.
I murmured, *I miss you,*
Hoping, trusting,
The slight summer breeze
Elegantly carried my words
Across the veil.

Poet Soup

I stir the simmering pot,
Add a bit of seasoning, spice,
Thrust in my ladle,
Fill my empty white bowl,
Then off, back to my ways,
Though, ever hungry, unsatisfied,
I am still not much the cook.

The Ministering Pine

Of this divine spot
Beneath the stretched shadows of
The majestic granite dome,
Have paths nursed my trail
To thee.

Leaning close, I breathe in
The scent of your perfumed needles,
Encamp my unsettled spirit here,
Exhale in the chill these doubts
That so burden me.

Then as the crow caws,
The stream hums,
Clouds drift across the sky,
You purely recite your
Lovely verse to me -

'Here it is that I shall ever be –
branching, flourishing, arching
toward the light - I shall neither wander
nor know of these aversions you speak
and suspicions that divide.'

And then with the dipping sun
Comes my farewell,
Realizing I will never see you again,
I delicately touch your green robe,
And you minister these parting lines to me -

'You be who you be, in these days that remain –
embrace the course, the joy of seasons gifted thee –
for thy path of thought, of love, of kindness, of hope
is never to be in me, but is there breathing for thee.'

June Emancipation

Stand on Chestnut Street,
Regard the sacred Philadelphia hall,
Celebrate those who pledged
Their lives and honor for liberty.
Yet the toll of the celebrated bell
Was muffled that July day.
The crack widened across her bronze innocence,
A lasting mark of imperfect union.
Make your way to 24th and Broadway
In Galveston away from crowds.
Gaze up at the balcony on the second floor.
Listen. Imagine. Pray.
Hear the scared Philadelphia bell
Ringing sounds of Emancipation!

Beneath

Shall we poke deeper down below the soil
With our shared ploughing pen?
Might we pause from that which we toil,
Explore beneath this flesh again?
Here, under, we cast aside temptations betrayal,
We smell the sweetness of our love's glen.

To the Hatchling

It is sobering that your mother
Has gracefully chosen here
Outside my bedroom window
To nurture your delicate beginnings.

I have seen her and she is strong,
Focused on nature's call.
I have whispered through the pane of glass
That her home is mine, as mine is hers.

As your wings wire and feathers form
With the rising light and warming sun,
I ponder how far from this nest
You shall sing your peaceful songs.

I smile imagining the alluring, flowering woods
Through which you will artfully glide.
Now, though, rest preciously here,
Into tomorrows you shall fly, be still, sweet creature today.

What of the Universe?

The belt of asteroids,
The spinning sphere,
Mountains of red rock,
Streaking comets
know not of their beauty,
Feel nothing of pain or grief,
Of love, faith, joy,
No sense of meaning for the tender touch.
For what would the universe be
Were it not for the soul within
That pauses to sing of it,
To write of it,
To paint it?

Farewell Royal Lady of Leamington

Today a gentle breeze
Crossed the River Leam.
Her delicate wings did spread,
She took flight,
Ever so softly brushing the stream,
Graceful ripples remained.
Farewell, I cried,
Dearest, kindest of souls.
I will forever search
The clouds for you.

A Party for the Departed

The card is in,
The flap is sealed,
Invite on its way.
No costumes required,
No shimmering gowns,
Put your pressed white shirts
And black ties away.
It is a rather unornamented gathering
Meant for those whom we miss,
The ones we love.
We shall convene independently,
Each hold a picture of them
Softly in hand,
Touch it.
We shall close our eyes and
Quietly utter a thought to them.
Please, do come.
Our spirits are bound together,
By this ache,
We share.

Warm Blanket

I stitch together the fabric emerald fields of
Perthshire to those of Virginia.
My heart the needle,
My fondness the thread.
I wrap this flowing cloak of warmth around me,
Covering myself from the chill of uncertainty
That seeps through the cracks of my troubled mind.
There is room, comfort underneath for you.
Come in.
We all tremble, shiver,
Need such soothing splendor.
Please, come in.

Letting Go

Watch me twist the clock back,
Pull out the plug, toss the batteries,
Click off the switch.
Yet, I cannot impede time.
I shall put my anxious hands down,
Open my aged eyes,
Cherish the soft chimes of
Earnest moments that
I have been given,
And gratefully watch it
Tick forward.

Moments Before Farewell

We have traveled far together,
Now from this elevated green hill we pause,
I look below and more clearly hear
The choir of sea birds singing
Hovering around the wooden stage
From which you shall raise your sail to the crisp breeze,
Lift anchor,
And ease away into the salted sea.
There is a weight in the thought,
Yet also a father's pride in the person
You have become, and are molding.
These final steps together with you still ashore
Are divinely gifted me, to us.

Sun Setting Days

The spirit of the dipping sun
Inspired me to drape my arm across
My life's most cherished friend,
"it has been a good life, a good life, indeed."

Above and Below the Sea

Tis here above the skin I breathe,
Yet beneath the layer
Is where my soul wades
To depths of dimming light,
Enveloping chills,
Pain is with me in this blackened deep.
'Learn from fear' calls out
the salted, muffled sea in me.
Then to this call
I ascend through the swells,
Burst out to the surface
With a heart that breathes again,
not for me, but for YOU.

The Monument to Noble Women

As my soul hastily rushes
From city place to place,
Here the etched statues of women
Slow me – nobly bring me to a STOP.
Their courage keeps me still!

Me, Gathered Ash

Here comes to rest the dogwood petal,
A lovely live lived.
What treasure be mine if I
Modestly sleep on this blanket of earth?
What delicate fortune I would hold
If the gathered ash that tis me
Could repose in thought
That I too was in life
What I was crafted to be.

The Summer Ball

Stamped with the breeze
Hath the golden invite arrived.
She so patiently hoped it would,
Just, at least, once more again.
Now here doth the spring willow
Excitedly lean down to bathe
Her flowing locks of green.
She prepares for the summer ball
That nears.
Beaks will beg,
Wings will spread,
Hearts will take flight.
Would I greed to ask
This beauty before me
For just one more season of dance?
May I hold her soft hand,
Watch her graciously glide across the floor
Of this spot of castled earth?

City Birds

Silence,
You voices that divide!
Despair shall never hush the city birds
Who sing of hopeful spring.
Cast aside that proclamation of melancholy,
Listen to these creatures teach
That *you,*
That *we,*
Shall rise
again.

Mustard Seed

Hold on to that faith in yourself,
Your loves,
Passion for kindness,
For charity.
Even if it be the size of a mustard seed,
That faith will obey you,
Take root,
Richly spring up in remarkable places
You could never imagine,
Never dream.

The Shephard's Gate

Strikingly crafted,
Tribute to historic triumph,
Theatrical arch of white limestone,
Splashes of gold,
Ornately chiseled words of praise.
The metropolis gate lures
Bustling masses,
Trinket sellers,
Throngs of urban lenses.
And here amidst the
Emerald Cumbrian fields,
Is old shepherd's gate,
Laid with modest means,
Everyday intent.
Rusted latches,
Weathering wood,
Sounds of chattering crowds,
Passing cars,
Are substituted with
Singing robins,
Unhurried sheep.

Farewell for Now

Your wide guileless eyes searched my lips,
Your keen mind churned over the words
I uttered over time.
As best I thought how, I modestly wove together
Scriptures of sanctity,
Passages of purity,
Words of wisdom,
All while shouldering
My own weaknesses
And personal doubts.
While goodness is that light to which I aspired,
Not always was I bravely sure in my step.
I spoke of honesty,
Then bowed to craftiness.
I proclaimed open your heart to others,
Then padlocked my own.
I acted out stories of charity,
Then penned selfish plays.
I sang melodies of love,
Then struck notes of apathy.
I praised sturdiness of character,
Then wobbled unworthily.

Perhaps not as deeply as I,
Yet, you knew, you witnessed in me
The cracking contradiction
That meanders across the father's complexion.
And now here we are poised,
Backs not fully erect,
Shouldering the human imperfections, we carry.
I am humbled by the reality of this moment,
The cleansing purity that sincere farewells stir.

Yet know that while I still have lingering doubts
Of which no soul entirely evades,
I feel liberty here.
I know many have come
To shape you, including you.
I place aside my weaknesses,
For through my faithful eyes
That well with pride, I see you who was
Once so wee, now the sterling knight,
Sparkling with stature before me,
A gentle and willing servant of God,
So dear,
Accepting,
Kind,
Noble,
Radiant,
So, loving and loved,
Cherished by me.

Her Matchless Beauty

Dear Ms. Austen (Jane),
Your words waltz elegantly across a ballroom of thought,
Stepping forward to me as the fiddle hums
In my late summer daydream.
I glance up and see there extended before me your open hand,
An unexpected invite to me.
Me? Me, whose stumbling sentences on such floors
Often keep me here seated,
The shyly cornered observer.
Yet, not today!
I grab hold of your hand with a glimmer in my eye,
This joyous party must know what I know
My coyness will rest and my freedom will dance.
I turn and twist telling you of her,
Her matchless beauty,
Her wisdom,
Forgiving way, vibrant grace.
Ah, what rejoicing there would be if you inked your quail again,
Wrote warm melodic passages of dearest, Jo.

Young Fallen

I would scrub your blackened warrior face.
Clean the burned cork, cocoa from your eyes.
I would sponge the dirt of war from your cheeks,
Move a soft towel across the red dreadful.
But too far from you do I stand,
I am powerless, but, for my silent bow.
Striking sun has this marker whitened,
Though not near beauty your handsome young life,
shortened.

The Shinning Heart

Shallow distractions too often pull me away,
Then you appear,
A smooth shimmer of kindness in your soul
That draws my eye from the ever-churning clutter,
A treasure untold,
Sweet pearl of fortune to hold.
There is nothing of greater value
Than the illuminating shine that is you.

Rising Light

The voice of the
Rising light,
Breathes through
The blossoming wood –
Here I am!
Pause in my embrace –
Draw from me what you might,
That peace you need to meet
Those storms ahead.
My white sheet is clean,
Shall I simply listen,
Put the ink away,
Spoil not sanctity,
For words in me would
Surely fall short,
again.

Homeless Night

Her sleep was intermittent,
Rest disrupted
Not by bedside alarms,
Neither the aroma of an awakening kitchen,
Nor even by the passing of glaring city sirens.
What kept her on the awoken edges
Was the silent sightless chill.
She was alone,
Hurting,
Hungry.
I saw it in her face
As the winds
Whipped against her
Plastic sheets of black.
Her spirit seemed to float
Away with the steam from grates
That surrounded her.
Hold on.
Homeless, sweet stranger,
Please, hold on through this frigid night.
Yet,
If you go,
Heaven will sing your welcome,
Your burden gone,
Your heart and hands warm again.

Emily

Was that your intrepid soul
That meandered down my
Window pain as morning broke,
Pulled me up and out?
Was it you who sweetly chirped
A wordless song
In the grey stillness,
Carpeted the earth in sprinkles of
Ginger and bronze crackling
Beneath my steps?
Was that you circling
The garden sowing
Seeds on the floor of the
Roofless cathedral,
Your face in the droplet
Embracing the scarlet berry?
I do believe it was you,
Gently guiding the flock of deer
With your delicate hand,
Still probing, still shaping,
Still pushing forward,
Now withdrawn only from
The lyric you feared,
The one I now so
imperfectly carry.

Below the Human Skin

I stand inches from the finely
Crafted armored suit
Once of Tudor legend,
KING HENRY VIII!
Dream do I of noble knights,
Alluring this shimmering jewel
Before me.
If the royal who wore this
Regal costume stood,
Granted me a moment to speak
Eye to eye, face to face,
Stand as equal and pose
Questions would I.
Were the victories of life found
On fields of conflict green?
Were triumphs uncovered
On open seas prowled by *Mary Rose*?
Did ever you attain wealth
Beneath this armor,
Nobility below the coat of
Human skin?

Aging Wall

Do not feel ashamed
Of your diminishing strength
So nakedly exposed
To those who pass.
You were chiseled for reason
And remain in place without boast
Having worked beneath
Years of shining sun.
You have endured
The howling winds,
Soaking rains,
Penetrating chills.
You have held firm,
Mightily borne the
Weight of countless seasons.
So, do not hold low,
Fret over winding cracks.
Hear my quiet
Celebration of your loveliness,
The wisdom that is now you.

Time Calls Out

I cannot elude you,
Though moments am I persuaded
By human pride, conveying,
See the foe!
I am the weak stoic of nature's truth.
Aging, I begin to resign.
I am no more than the leaf blown to
The garden floor,
The crevasse shell in the trenches of
The sea,
Ants scurrying beneath mountain rock.
I am no more than the ash
Of a burned forest tree.
Yet, my resignation
Neither admits defeat
Nor overshadows my gratitude.
I am forever alive in you!
I stand tall knowing that I occupy
The same stage as light itself
Streaming across the distant reaches of universe.
I know as tides of shadows ebb and flow,
You are calling out to me, to all,
Embrace the gifted moment, you say,
Comfort the verses of others who, too,
Have been granted this space
To grow, to roam,
To be.

You, The Painting

I have pulled closer
Than most to you,
Seen the cracking of
Seemingly bland
White and grey brush strokes.
That narrow focus will prompt
Some to say, see the imperfection,
The dullness of the complexion.
Impatient they turn, walk away,
In search of something perceived
More glamorous.
Trust that I will never do.
I embrace those textures and colors in you.
I know it is what makes your soul
Beautifully human.
And, while I will never depart,
I will occasionally step back,
Admire a wider perspective
That also reminds me of the
Framed golden elegance,
Polished grace,
The painting that is
You.

She, Antonia

Giacomo long toiled forlorn in artful figurative stucco,
Weary of creating for the small Sicilian church,
His soul bearing the weight of personal fiasco,
An aimless aging sculptor, life in unsteady lurch.

Antonia was the shepherd's matured daughter from Palermo,
Often venturing alone to softly pray, to search,
Her words, her thoughts the graceful heavenly echo,
Pews her resting place, her chosen angelic perch.

Seemingly desirous no more, Giacomo added gloom thereto,
Then sighted Antonia's light streaming beneath the arch,
Above her black hair rested a redemptive halo,
Lifting that which caused his heart to parch.

Renovation Splendor

The brass colored doorways of
St. Patrick's Cathedral
Are cast widely open,
Drawing in many of the throng,
Tinted clad souls passing at Christmas.
Inside, amidst the consistent hymn of
Muffled voices, clicking cameras,
Deliberate flow of squeaking shoes,
There are those who solitarily sit,
Clasp their hands,
Bow their heads,
Whisper,
Kneel,
Reflect upon matters of
Joy,
Sacrifice,
Family, loss, sorrow,
Forgiveness.
And there surrounding them
In this venerable monument of peace
Is an answer in the form of
Crossing steel tubes of shining silver scaffolding,
Skilled engineering platforms,
Colored cords,
Construction helmets crowning expertise,
Buzzing drills, erect ladders,
Orange cones, whistling saw blades,
Pounding hammers.
Renovation rings! It vigorously sings!
A sign mentions it is *temporary*, but *necessary*.
And so, it is with those burdened souls
Here, like me, this season seeking rest,

Relief, pity, strength.
The work of renovation is gracefully spinning
And polishing within us.
Necessary to life,
Our pain will be eased,
Our purpose and joy restored
To its original splendor.

Carmel Cypress

I still roam, often search, absorb the load of lingering doubt
Through a winding, dusty journey of discovery
Within myself embarked upon so long ago.
It was necessary and remains so. Your needs are different.
As I continue to stir, shift, find truth, discard vanity along the way,
I have felt the stones beneath my now tattered feet,
The early dash has evolved
To a set of deliberate, softer steps.
I admire you for that which
I will never completely acquire
But continuously seek,
Your perfect understanding
Of why you are firmly
Rooted on that solitary
Spot of holy earth,
Reaching to the light
With no want
Of doubt to
Explore.

The Coventry Girl

There was no youthful
On the bustling corner,
No hands aloft holding enlarged ink headlines,
Absent the procession of scarlet clad guard
Upon regal horses prancing down Spon
Passing closed shops.
No tower bells ringing from Coventry's Cathedral
Through the winter chill.
No shinning brass trumpets or royal address.
But on this day, *Agnes,* a princess, was born.
As the eyes of the world looked elsewhere,
Angels authored in her tired mother's ear,
Stirred in her anxious father's heart,
A carol of how God had brought
To their modest Christmas home
A singular daughter
Who would crown her life
With boldness and grace.

Hand in Stream

I so effortlessly break through
The thin layer of
Glimmering glass,
My hand,
My soul,
Awoken to the soothing residue of
Once a winter snow now
Rushing by.

As effortlessly as I reached in,
I lift out,
Close my eyes,
Cool my aging face.
The breeze,
The summer air,
Towels drying
My human face.

Tranquil, humbled,
I open my eyes
To a legion of
Angels cloaked
In green, blue,
Red, white,
All singing notes from
Heaven's pages.

The celebrated gift of life
Had been opened
For me long ago.
Time is more precious
And fleeting now.
Why now to possess this
Mortal hand to dip in
This stream?

The Fisher's Alter

Out to North Sea, Nellie did rarely rest to look,
Never traveling, she knew but one and only place, Anstruther.
This coastal lass accepted the hardened life of East Neuk,
Fishing was the net gathering her past, present, and future.

The frigid evening before Rabbie departed for fish to hook,
Rain battered his harboured Scaffie, fists of wind unrelenting bruiser.
Nellie held their bairns, eased their tidy hearts that shook,
The couple had become, together, the convincing and humble soother.

Stirring a simmering scran broth that only she could cook,
Nellie settled the family, they bowed heads to a ruler.
Rabbie said to Nellie, if ever his love she mistook,
That his prayers had been answered as her loving suitor.

Day was normal into dusk, then the startling door knock,
The man in cloth spoke words to Nellie in blur.
Rabbie had slipped into the stormy sea from the boat's deck,
Heartbroken love, Fife breasts, again, prey for the fisher's alter.

Change

Change looms in the swirling breeze,
Rustling what seemed motionless for so long.
Doubt creeps in and blocks the light above,
Still it is there!
I feel it.
I see it flicker.
A glimmer of certainty,
Even while dear innocence
Sways in the wind.

The Stage

The light slowly fades in.
Upon stunning morning elegance
It shines across the garden stage.
To serene setting characters enter.
The fox eases in, stops, anxiously scurries away,
Wrens sing harmonious notes,
Squirrels dance with energetic flair,
A dog barks in the distance.
I sit on a rock, listen, eyes alert.
Am I of the audience or
Mishandling my part?

The Chorister

"Is to-day nothing?
Is the beginningless past nothing?
If the future is nothing,
they are just as surely nothing."
The rays of light from your words
Beam forward to my soul.
The past sings her hymn,
You are the chorister!

Humility of Snow

I sing of humility
When a fulfilling smile
Spans her face.
Submissive am I when her hands
Open spilling white diamonds of
Grandeur below.

We Are More

If we were but once
And no more
Single cascading drips
From the cliff's edge,
What thrill in life there be,
Splendor so complete –
No need to add.
Ah, but what joy
To know we are and have been granted
Souls of so much more!

Winter Meets Spring

It is not often
The blooming dogwood
In early splendor
Meets the white snow,
When ice flakes present
Themselves to innocent red blossoms
Ignorant of this once legend chill.
But when gatherings do occur,
A precious friendship
Between old and new
Stirs my heart,
What precious song
Have I witnessed tonight.

Blooming Ballet of Spring

Into the season's ballet
You enter with a soundless flutter,
A pink pointe shoe
Delicate on stage.
Angels pause,
Motionless,
Catch their breath,
Gather hopeful strength
From the tantalizing dance
That is always you.

Sailing Ahead

Your creaking bow
Bound forward,
A laboring hull,
Rusted sword thrust
Into the currents of
The potent sea.
I, too, steer the open blue,
Proudly jutting along,
Horn boasting, look at me!
I am grander, finer,
Than you would ever be.
Then I lose my course,
Anxiously lost to land.
Turning, I see the modest
Wake you left,
I follow it,
Seeing again the
Bobbing speck of shore.
The gust whispers to me,
'it was she who selflessly
sailed ahead
for you.'

Anne's Beauty

I touch the fallen leaves, breathe in the air,
Think of you as I turn to the flower in bloom.
Again to me you visit with charm.
I witness the birds that glide on the wind,
Winged cousins of whom you delightfully wrote.
Lovely your ink that styled the shining, the silver rain,
Down from my window this morning,
Sisters, matching droplets that did streak.
My eyes meet the same sky you saw,
Gaze upon the arching tree,
Just as yours upon the Chestnut peered.
Shame those goons of rotten hearts,
Monsters who stole from the world
Unwritten novels, robbed us of your reflective pen,
Unforgotten their vicious crime upon the innocents.
So far in time and place are you and I removed,
Some will say how different we are,
Though proudly drawn to you shall I always be,
Your teenage light, your innocent fire
Shines and warmly kindles in me.
What gift can I, can we, possibly give
In return to you?

Durham Plea to Dark

I stand on Prebends Bridge in winter chill,
The bright chested robin sings notes to please,
A pure blue-sky rests behind the leafless trees,
Here downstream River Wear fills the hallow of my quill.

Yet, I am in doubt, sharp gloom cuts my onward will,
From my breast does despair out tease,
Wounds linger, pain circles round hope to seize,
From my eye does a tear again begin to spill.

Why darkness do you persist in finding to me a trail?
Once I'd climb 325 tower steps away from you to flee.
No longer do I wish to struggle you that asserts I fail,
May we in Durham splendor style peace, accept my aging plea?
Surely, so familiar to you my heart is now often frail,
If with me you shall stay, to the child yonder, please be free.

What We Have Gained

I still miss you, terribly,
Especially when pausing here
In Northern California,
Once home,
The spaces we together knew.

In those days of your passing
My quiet sorrow penetrated down
To a core of dark earth
Not known to me.
You were gone.

An alluring voice still whispers,
Asking if it could be so,
Would I cover my pained breast
To walk this ground again with you?
A tempting stroll, indeed.

Then a solitary crow floats
Across the hill.
I see a track of words feathered by its wings.
Grief is real the trail reads,
Though cherish this gift of his passing.

I know now better what I,
What we, have gained.
I'll carry the wisdom to places still.
Beyond this earth we shall be together again,
Until then, until then, Dearest Dad.

This Same

This same wind stirred
The face of the ocean,
Blew across the golden prairie.
This same wind shrilled
Across the mountain top,
Gusted against the sheep folding.
This same wind on my lips
Touches the cheek of another.

This same love traveled
The heart of the soul,
Drove passion to fresh joy.
This same love whistled
Across the mind highest,
Collided against the human shell.
This same love in my heart,
Touches the life of another.

Forgiving, One

I never heard the flowers bud
Nor the Robin build her nest.
I did hear you say with humility,
Please, please forgive me,
And you harkened from me the same,
With equal meekness.
A new season, we said together,
With welcoming hearts,
A fresh beginning to grow, to change.
Like the golden and crimson
Flowers unspoken bloom,
We uttered no more,
Simply holding close,
Imperfectly perfect as
one.

Labor Song

They arose before
Their children,
And were gone before
The rays of the morning sun
Could mark their distant journey.

They returned aching,
Grimy, hungry,
But still honest
And with a kind prayer
In their hearts.

They shouldered more
Than most ever could.
They did so time after time,
Clocking in and out
for far too little wage.

Still, they did it with pride!
They quietly labored
For country, community, family,
In search of a brighter,
Safer tomorrow.

Complexion Light

There was the grace of the sun
Stretching across the heavens
Resting on the face of the radiant moon.
The scene, the light, coupled me to you.
Grateful was I when together
We walked this life and I beheld
Such rays glimmer on your cheek,
Glisten in your eye.
I speak to you here in the winter night chill,
Long since we have parted,
Now, I journey alone.
I know there is more than me,
Many more lovers than we.
My breast does warm to think
What complexions the light
Shall gently brighten tonight.
Whose embraced hands strolling in a wood
Will it enliven in vivid blue?
For me, I smile here, thinking of you.

Settled

Standing on the corner in still morning dark before the sun rose,
I watched from a distance as heart and mind, two parts of me, debated in the
Fog beneath the shining street light.

Easing closer, they heard my clumsy steps, faces turned, eyes froze.
I knew not what at first to say, extended my hand and placed theirs in mine,
Holding each tight.

I acknowledged their uneasy exchange, saying they'd need not be foes.
We settled together there, our life is precious short, and wasted days we Would
if mired in ongoing fight.

Boarding Late Bus

The approaching bus he sought,
Standing alone with none to chat.
His heart still so fraught,
A yearning soul today so flat.

Am I forsaken, he thought?
Then he blearily boarded and sat.
Shall I pity this lot?
Then he pulled off his hat.

Life, what have I bought?
Then such beauty his eyes begat,
Lovingly pulling him from his wrought,
Notes from his Love did that.

Baby Daughter Joy

He so delicately
Embraced her,
Held her beauty in place.
She brought smoothness,
Purpose to his coarse edges.
A treasured,
Peaceful instant
Known just to them.
It was their precious spot
Of time together.
In this his boundless joy,
Her glittering eyes reflected
The light of heaven
As only this darling could.

I Am of The City Masses

I am of the city masses,
Rowing up and down asphalt streams,
Encircled by the stops and starts of purring steel,
Silver snakes curl through the chiseled
Darkness beneath my feet.

I am of the city masses,
Sculling past concrete forests,
Surveying flickering stars of red and green,
Throngs of vibrantly shelled four-legged beasts growl,
Seemingly ready to pounce on me.

I am of the city masses,
Charting my peculiar course through the snarled maze,
Paddling through the dense rains,
Navigating to elude the jungle's infectious disease
That so often like-minded souls succumb.

Mountain Side

Silver birds dangle from her ears,
Rocky paths wrinkle across her cheeks,
Her shoulders do delicately curve,
Hazel are her eyes,
Freckles dot her skin.
Those ancient, fair golden locks still do romance me,
Welcome always does she my lowly soul with soft touch.
She is the wise, honest, noble mountain side,
The elegant angel of my ever so fleeting walk.

Heart Bruised

My candle burned deep into blackened night.
I wrestled swirling demons with ardent might,
Praying they'd parish in flickering light.
When morning rose my heart was bruised, contrite,
Goodness had prevailed over spite.
I wobbled up, yearning my soul would now bend right.

Behind the Castled Silhouette

The castled walls
Of your silhouette
Are striking, take the
Breath of many away.
Yet I discern
Stirring behind
The stacked grey stone
Are colorful brushes
Of a shy, penetrable
Soul. It is here that you
May trust that I
Shall protect you as
The royal you are.

The DACOR Bacon Gem

Again, I arrive at the pearl on 1801 F Street,
The four-story façade of red brick does cordially greet.
Up the six steps I stride past the flowers in bloom,
Such loveliness dost cast aside the heart's traces of gloom.

Through the grand white door, I humbly enter, gentle.
Permit modest me into a house, to history so instrumental?
Each visit does some story inspire, certain needs in me touches,
Reaches out to pour a pleasure that my spirit catches.

There the finger on the cheek of Lady Dunmore in soft repose,
The aging desk of Adams on which he wrote diplomatic prose.
See the piano keys that Rubinstein's hands artfully brushed,
The mature leather books, pages across a reader never rushed.

Under delicate smile of young Virginia Murray in blue dress,
I stand with my Foreign Service friends, countless do impress.
I scan chiseled corners, edges crafted by carpenters nameless,
What splendor shaped in this home by the laboring fameless.

I yearn to ponder in the serene garden on a steady basis,
To rest my fragile soul ever in need of such a nurturing oasis.
I witness a sweet bird perch high upon the regal courtyard tree,
To her singing songs of melodic invitation, I accept in full glee.

Tenderly

He suffered from a prolonged drought
Of joy.
He pleaded that the clouds would
Again open.
Yet, the moisture of simple pleasure
Was allusive.
His diminishing hope gradually turned to
Hardened earth.
He turned to ideas of slumber,
Forever sleep.
Then came the droplet streaming down
His cheek,
To quivering lips came tastes of
His frailty.
Then she touched sweet love,
His face, tenderly.

Summer

And so
Under the bridge
Passes another summer,
Until in its ancient splendor
It shall resplendently return again.

Mother, Father

I heard you
This morning
Whispering in the wind,
Singing with the birds.
I saw you peeking,
Reaching through
The clouds down
To me with an
Encouraging ray,
A warming, calm touch.
You shall always be with me.

Somber Night

Many a somber night her glow
Has been the guiding,
Soothing light.
I have seen my regretful
Breath of words
Bring her flame
To a flicker.
Yet, through my
Selfish breeze
She still reassuringly gleams.
She softly radiates
Not for her,
But for me,
For others.
The one who often stretches
Harmful shadows is me,
She bows to a faith
In kindness.
That sweet bright ardor
Which sways in her
Is what gives goodness
A brilliant path
Through this darkness of
Mine.

You, Captain, at the Helm

Your meditations have been ferried from
The bustling Brooklyn shores,
Blown without fare across rivers of time,
Navigating to humbled me standing alone in
The hushed chill of a golden wood.
My dear friend,
Oh, my captain,
I securely moor your thoughts,
Anchor your soft nursing soul here with me.
Roll call, commence!
Count me among the generations hence,
The loving living crowd of your past imagination.
Know me as a shipmate tied to you,
Part of that disintegrated scheme,
Yet, one who hears and sings your song of similitude.
You once heard as I
The winter winds whip through trees
As the rising sun beamed from the east.
There is the elegant ballet of swaying branches,
The chirping wren seeking companionship,
The anxious squirrel who gathers,
Geese in artful formation soaring across a canvas of blue.
I know these all and more were to you cherished,
As they are to me.
Life was yours, is fleetingly mine,
Vigor shall be in the hearts of those yet to sail.
I do not possess the same talents
To place stately leaves on grass,
So, I shall pilot forward with you at the helm,
Me, a modest sailor,
Alongside many crew who will journey by your side
When that future soul many years removed
shall kindly welcome us at port.

July 20, 1969

Joe gazed up at the bright burning moon,
His rifle functioning, fully loaded,
His soul broken, long since empty.
He was the private, damp in the Vietnamese jungle,
The drafted 19-year-old teenager from inner Detroit.
Officers had said that day that astronauts walked on the moon!
The clouds blew in, blanketed the humid night sky,
Drenching rains came to visit again,
A letter he started for his mother now soggy paper washed away.
The platoon tried to rest, though always anxious,
Fear did govern the nights.
The rain abated, the evening sky cleared,
Then the fire fight landed with surprise to all.
Joe took one small hesitant step, then a giant leap into the clash,
He felt the muddied surface slip under his boot, was hit twice,
Dying right there, the lunar light shown above him
Laying lifeless in the grass.
Mankind's eyes were turned elsewhere,
Tranquil angels not so, knowing an innocent
Eagle, a feather of God, had landed to his rest.

I Shall Not Flee

Once early on
I was the summer flower,
Vibrant in full bloom.
As we drew nearer,
My peddles fell,
My colors dimmed,
Imperfections in me exposed.
I was not what I appeared
At first to be.
I then became afraid at what you
Would do with me.
Then to ease my distress, you said,
'Have no fear,
I shall not flee,
Across the seasons you shall
Always be the choicest flower
To me.'

Newlyn Petals Shine Red

Four men gathered by the Newlyn War Memorial statue on Strand,
They contently gobbled lunch, chatted on benches green.

Fish and chips, a West Country staple fed this unassuming local band,
Seagulls circled, squawked, perched nearby for wasted scraps they did glean.

The men knew many valiant died for Cornish values, sacrificed for this land,
Poppies dotted tributes, sea rays illuminated petals red, grace won the scene.

The Proud Refugee

Do you these many years hence remember once malnourished, helpless me?
I was the infant girl held under the courageous mother's arm.

I, born of war-torn parents who from Aleppo did fearfully flee,
Such cavernous hatred, hearts failed, people suffered unspeakable harm.

We traversed barren land, boarded inflatable boats, crossing perilous sea,
Our stomachs empty, sickness replete, our eyes burning with alarm.

We came to Turkey, Greece, Germany, then finally Scotland to be,
I came first to Clackmannanshire, families kind, homes so warm.

I now stand tall! The graduate, the leader, the voice, The Proud Refugee!
Yes, I was the infant girl held under the courageous mother's arm.

Autumn Last

These the final days, my life's autumn last
Whiffing spices before the winter dims.
Content, request no more of seasons past,
I sing the notes of celebration hymns.

Watch the lone pink daisy in final bloom,
The chattering crow a harvest does scan,
I bow to fragrant air, how life passed to doom,
Love I felt profound, shame when from I ran.

In morning haze, I peel back my false mask,
The truthful rays do cheer my soul once gray.
A subtle breeze beckons my eyes to task,
Dipping to earth vibrant colors portray.

Stretching shadows embrace my gratitude,
I breathe deep on the verge of solitude.